W

HOOTON — BADGER'S
SHOTWICK — WOODB

DISTANCE:— 9 miles ... ½ Hours

START:— Hooton Railway Station **O.S. Ref:—** SJ/349/782

This walk is through the dairy-cattle country of South Wirral.

On emerging from Hooton Railway Station, turn left and climb up the steps to the road. Walk to the left over the bridge, and turn left down a second flight of steps on to the Wirral Way path, signposted "To Willaston".

Go forward to cross the disused platform of the old Birkenhead-West Kirby railway (1a), and continue ahead, tracing the direction in which the railway used to run.

After about ¾ mile, one passes through a gateway, and 100 yards further on, through a second gateway and under an arch. About 20yds further, turn right along the broad track, ignoring the signpost ahead of you.

Proceed along this track for 100yds to a tarmac road. At the road, turn right, and walk uphill to pass over the humped bridge.

Go forward, passing a poultry farm on the left, to reach a junction. Here, bear right on to a track signposted "Bridleway". This track leads to Oaks Farm.

Pass between the farm buildings, and continue ahead, passing through the gateway, on to a tree-lined lane. After ½mile, one reaches a crossroads. Ignoring the fieldpath sign on the right, go forward a few yards and turn right into a lane signposted "Hallwood Farm".

Go forward, and a small wood soon comes into view. Continue along the lane through a gateway, passing the houses, and then between the end-buildings, with the riding stables at the left, and forward to the field.

Bear slightly right at the field-edge, passing through a gateway, and walk forward across the field, keeping to the right-hand hedge, along a faint stony track to a gateway.

On passing through the gateway, bear right, along the track for 50yds to a solitary tree. Here bear left across the field to a tree at the end of the hedge ahead. Go forward, with the hedge on your left, across the next field to a stile. Cross the stile, and go forward through a bachelor-gate to the main A540 road, crossing any cattle-wire.

Turn left along the main road, and pass Badger's Rake House. At the junction, go forward across Badger's Rake Lane, and on reaching the bus stop at the house, carefully cross the dual-carriageway, and enter a path signposted "Puddington".

Proceed along the right-hand hedge of the first field, to cross a footbridge. Go directly forward to a curved-edged wood, crossing any cattle-wire. Bear left along the hedge to reach a metal stile in the corner.

Cross the stile and go forward to circumnavigate a pond to your left, and then cross the stile at the right of the gateway. In the next field, bear right and across, along the line of telegraph poles to a stile, which is crossed to enter a wooded path.

This path emerges in an earthy lane, which is followed downhill for a mile, to reach the village of Puddington (1b), the Welsh hills being visible directly ahead across the River Dee.

At the telephone box on the village green, cross to the pavement opposite, and using this, keeping the houses on your right, begin the journey to Shotwick, going uphill past West Hall to a T-junction. Here, turn right, into a lane signposted "Shotwick".

Go forward past a group of houses (do **not** turn right), on to a grassy lane ahead. This leads to a cattle-grid, alongside of which is the signposted path to Shotwick (1c).

Pass through the gate at the right of the grid, and cross the field diagonally leftwards to the far hedge, where a track leads downhill to a second field. Cross this field diagonally to the right, to the end of the hedge opposite.

With the pond on your left side, go again diagonally right, under the electricity cables to the hedge, where the path leads downhill, the Dee Marshes being visible ahead.

At the field-corner, pass left through a pair of gates. Keep to the right-hand hedge, and pass over a shallow ditch, through a gate to a grassy track. This track emerges at a farm.

Country Walks on Merseyside

by

David Parry

Cover Design: Eric R. Monks
Maps by the Author

First published 1988 by Countyvise Limited, 1 & 3 Grove Road, Rock Ferry, Birkenhead, Wirral, Merseyside L42 3XS.

Photoset and printed by Birkenhead Press Limited, 1 & 3 Grove Road, Rock Ferry, Birkenhead, Merseyside L42 3XS.

ISBN 0 907768 24 5.

CONTENTS

INTRODUCTION

The walks in this book start and finish within or near the Merseyside Transport area.

They are along public footpaths, fieldpaths, country lanes, and canal towing-paths.

The route of each walk is accompanied by a sketch-map. The maps are not drawn to scale, but should help in following the route.

Places of special interest are labelled with numbers, which relate to footnotes below the description of each walk.

Public Transport information appears in a separate section.

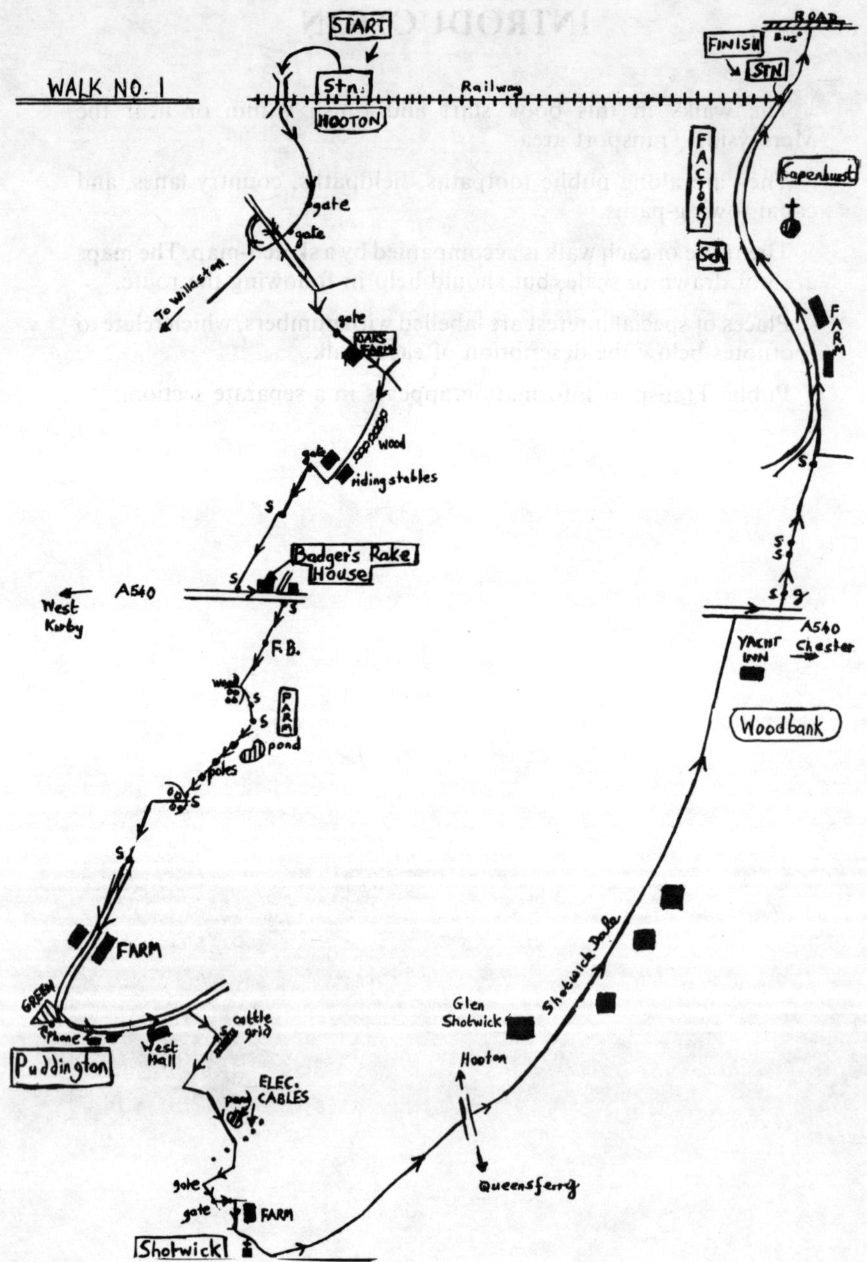
WALK NO. 1
START
Stn.
HOOTON
Railway
gate
gate
To Willaston
gate
OAKS FARM
wood
gate
riding stables
S
Badger's Rake House
S
A540
West Kirby
S
F.B.
wood
S
FARM
S
pond
poles
S
S
FARM
GREEN
Phone
West Hall
Puddington
cattle grid
ELEC. CABLES
pond
gate
gate
FARM
Shotwick
Hooton
Queensferry
Glen Shotwick
Shotwick Dale
Woodbank
YACHT INN
A540
Chester
S
g
S
S
S
FARM
Sch
FACTORY
Capenhurst
FINISH
STN
Bus
ROAD

Bear right, and pass the barns. Then take the 2nd-left turn, downhill along the lane, past Shotwick Hall, and forward into the village. A right turn takes you to the ancient Shotwick Church (1d).

At the churchyard gates, leave Shotwick by going forward, keeping the houses to your right, past the derestriction signposts, the road curving slightly to the left, and then down to the main Hooton-Queensferry road.

Carefully cross the road, and enter the narrow lane directly opposite — this is the road to Woodbank. Go forward uphill, passing Glen Shotwick and Shotwick Dale on the left, and then a number of large houses on the right. After the hill-top is reached, a mile of easy walking leads to the Yacht Inn at Woodbank.

The final stage of our journey, to Capenhurst, begins at the Yacht Inn. The main A540 road is crossed, and then one turns right, in the direction of Chester, for 100 yds only. Pass the houses and the post-box, and then turn left on to a field-path through a stiled gateway.

Go over the field and cross a double stile at the foot of the large tree. Cross the field along the left hedge to a gate and stile, over which one emerges on to the Capenhurst road.

Go forward along the tarmac road towards Capenhurst, carefully using the right-hand grass verge. After a mile, one reaches Capenhurst village green at Rectory Lane, and just further on, the church and school.

Continuing along the left-hand pavement, we pass the factory, to reach our journey's end at Capenhurst Railway Station, via the narrow lane on the left, for trains to Hooton and Liverpool.

Should the station be closed on Sundays, one crosses the humped bridge over the railway, and goes forward to the main Birkenhead road, where a bus can be boarded.

1a. THE BIRKENHEAD-WEST KIRBY RAILWAY

The line was opened from Hooton to Parkgate in 1866. The main reason for its construction was the transport of coal from a colliery at Neston to Birkenhead, via Hooton, and also through Hooton to Chester and beyond. The line was extended to West Kirby in 1886. The railway was single-tracked and there were turntables at West Kirby and at Hooton. The twelve-mile stretch from Hooton to West Kirby was closed to passenger traffic in 1956, and to goods traffic in 1962.

The railway track was removed, and later a footpath was laid down, which is now known as the Wirral Way. It was opened to the public in 1973, and together with its associated side-paths, forms the Wirral Country Park.

1b. PUDDINGTON

The village of Puddington was in existence in Norman times. The manor was held by the Massey family from those times until 1795. The family seat was later demolished, and Puddington Hall, which is situated between the village green and the River Dee, is a building of a later date.

Following the Battle of Preston during the Stuart Rebellion, William Massey was captured at Puddington, and taken to Chester Castle, where he was imprisoned until his death a year later.

1c. SHOTWICK

The village was in ancient times a place from which passage was possible, via a ford and a ferry, across the River Dee into Wales. Ships could dock at Shotwick, and like Parkgate, a little further north-east along the Dee shore, passages to Ireland could be started from a quay.

The continuous silting-up of the estuary brought about a diversion of the tideway by the cutting of a canalised section, which runs from Chester to near Connah's Quay on the Welsh shore. The "New Dee Cut" was completed in 1725, and the river no longer laps against the walls of Shotwick church.

Shotwick was a village set on the old "Saltesway", a trading route for the transport of salt dug from the Cheshire deposits around Winsford, and for many years the road to Shotwick was a highway for the passage of the English armies into Wales. King Henry III passed through Shotwick with his army in 1245, as did Edward I in 1278 and in 1284.

In the 17th century, Shotwick underwent many changes. In 1641 the plague visited the village, claiming many, who were then buried in the churchyard. Following the Civil War, many of the houses were rebuilt, and these, together with some of the farm-buildings, date from that time.

1d. SHOTWICK CHURCH

The Domesday Book tells us that at the time of its compilation a church existed at "Sotowiche". It is known that in 1093 the church was in the possession of the Benedictine monks of St. Werburgh's Abbey at Chester, which later became the city's cathedral. At this time, the Abbey was rebuilt, as was Shotwick church. Many alterations have been made to the church. It was rebuilt and extended during the 14th and 15th centuries.

The tower dates from the 16th century, and the clock was installed in 1726. The present roof was built in 1871. The masonry of the porch contains grooves, believed to have been worn away by villagers sharpening their arrows before practising archery after the Sunday services.

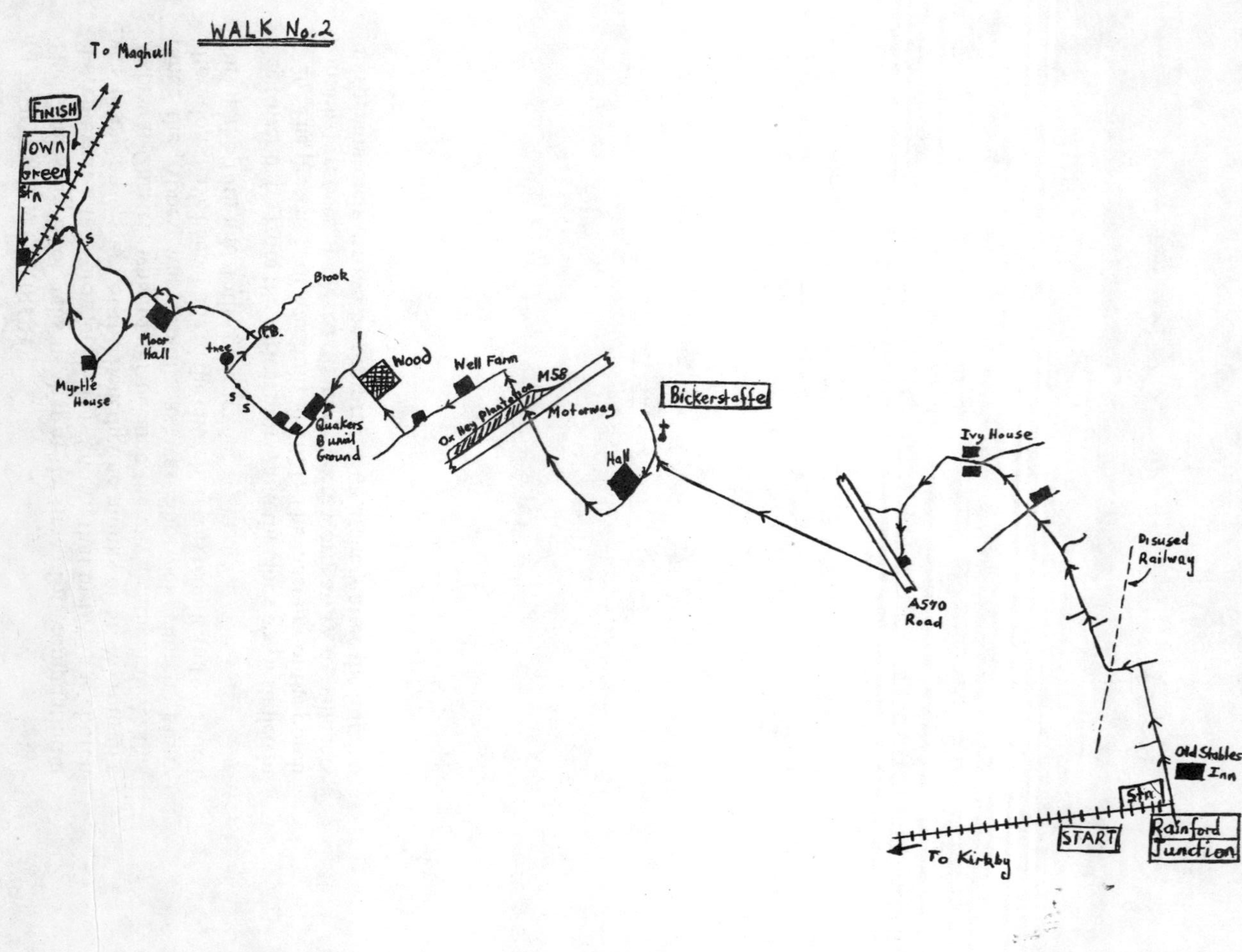

WALK No. 2
To Maghull
FINISH
Town Green
Stn
S
Myrtle House
Moor Hall
Brook
F.B.
tree
S
S
Quakers Burial Ground
Wood
Well Farm
Ox Hey Plantation
M58
Motorway
Bickerstaffe
Hall
Ivy House
A570 Road
Disused Railway
Old Stables Inn
Stn
START
Rainford Junction
To Kirkby

WALK No. 2

RAINFORD — BICKERSTAFFE — AUGHTON TOWN GREEN

DISTANCE:— 8 Miles **ALLOW:—** 5½ Hours

START:— Rainford Junction Station **O.S. Ref:—** SD/478/026

This walk crosses the fertile land of the Lancashire Plain.

Opposite the "Old Stables" inn at Rainford Junction station (2a), turn left, and pass along News Lane for ¼ mile in the direction of Skelmersdale. At the road junction, go forward towards the open country ahead.

At the point where the road bends sharply to the right, turn left to leave the road along a track past the remains of a disused railway bridge (2b), and then turn right, and follow the path along the hedge to reach a lane. Here, bear left, and continue along the tarmac for a mile or so, to reach a T-junction.

Cross straight over, and enter a fieldpath at the right of the trees ahead, passing between the trees and the farm-paddock. Go forward, keeping to the left hedge and ditch, until, after passing through a second field, one goes forward along a track, and then between the buildings of Ivy House Farm.

On reaching the tarmac lane, the view at the horizon includes Bickerstaffe church and its adjoining woodland.

To continue the journey to Bickerstaffe, descend via the left-hand fork, to reach the main A570 road at the red-brick house. Cross the road to a signposted footpath in front of you, and follow this straight path between the field boundaries for a mile or so in the direction of the church steeple. The path widens to a track, before reaching the village of Bickerstaffe.

At the church gate, turn left, and then go right, along Hall Lane, past the school, the large barns, and the gates of Bickerstaffe Hall, then continue along the pavement, and turn right on to a signposted track.

Pass the side of the house, and go directly forward to the footbridge over the motorway, keeping to the left of the hedgerow. Cross the footbridge, turn left and then pass over Bickerstaffe Brook.

Go forward along the fence of the sewage works on to a track, and onwards, through a gateway to a road. Here, turn left, and walk down the left-hand pavement.

After ¼ mile, pass Well Farm, with the stretch of woodland known as Ox Hey Plantation along your left side.

After passing the next solitary building, look for a footpath on your right, situated between the telegraph poles, where the road begins to curve to the right. (An old signpost indicates where the path begins).

Cross the road and take to this path. Keeping to the right-hand side of the hedge, aim for the left edge of the wood visible ahead of you, being undeterred by any overgrowth of grass on the pathway.

On reaching the edge of the wood, keep on, with the length of the wood-edge alongside you as your guide.

On reaching the end of the tree-line, cross the next field along an old track, keeping the hedge to the left of you. After emerging at the lane, turn left, and walk towards the circle of pine trees.

The trees encircle the ancient Quakers' Burial Ground (2c).

Turn right, passing the houses and then Graveyard Farm. Continue along the track, and cross two metal stiles to reach a large tree. Here, bear slightly to the right for 20 yards, cross the footbridge on your left, and go forward across the field, along the right-hand hedgerow all the way.

The grassy path curves slowly leftwards to a lane, alongside a wood. Follow this lane for about 100 yards, and then follow the public footpath sign, going along the hedgerow, skirting the grounds of Moor Hall, and emerging at a lane. Here, turn right, and after about 200 yards, reach a main road.

Cross the road and turn left. Pass the entrance of Moor Hall, and walk along the main road pavement for about ¼ mile.

Turn right, on to a track alongside Myrtle Hall, and go forward in the direction of the telegraph poles, along the boundary of the housing estate, with the farmland on your left.

Follow this well-worn path, passing between the houses, along an avenue of trees, to emerge at a road.

Here, bear left and then take the first turning on the left, and walk down, past the Town Green Inn, to complete the walk at the railway station.

2a. RAINFORD

The village was at one time involved in the manufacture of firebricks and crucibles, making use of the clay beds in the locality. The Rainford Potteries concern was set up in 1890, for the manufacture of earthenware drainage pipes.

For a period of 20 years, up to the outbreak of the First World War, Rainford was a centre for the manufacture of clay tobacco pipes, and several collieries were in operation.

2b. THE OLD RAILWAY

The railway line ran between St. Helens and Ormskirk. A section of the line south of Rainford Junction station now forms a footpath in an area known as the Rainford Linear Park.

2c. THE QUAKERS' BURIAL GROUND

The Society of Friends had a Meeting House at Stanley Gate in Bickerstaffe. It was closed in 1786 and converted into cottages.

In 1661 a Quaker, Oliver Atherton, refused to pay tithes to the Countess of Derby, who was the lay rector of the parish. He was imprisoned and died there two years later. His supporters carried his corpse on a toùr of various Lancashire towns, where notices were nailed up, stating that he had been "persecuted to death for keeping a good conscience". His remains were then interred in the Burial Ground.

Walk No 3

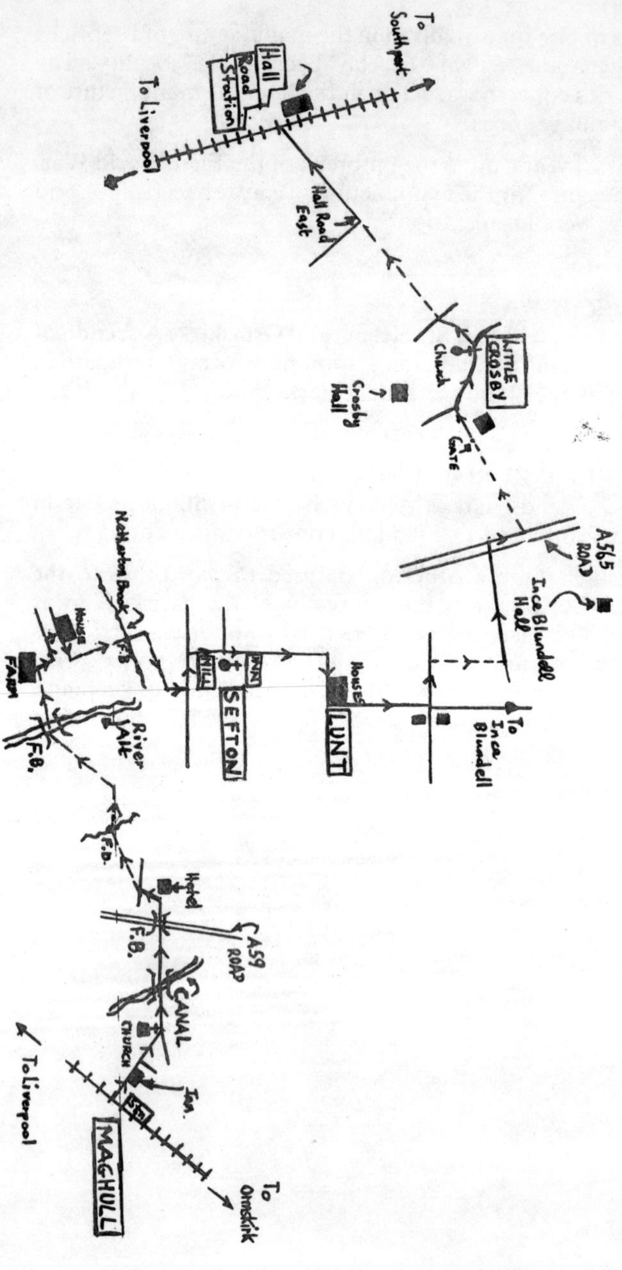

To Southport
To Liverpool
Hall Road Station
Hall Road East
LITTLE CROSBY
Church
Crosby Hall
GATE
A565 ROAD
Ince Blundell Hall
To Ince Blundell
HOUSES
LUNT
INN
SEFTON
Netherton Brook
HOUSE
F.B
FARM
River Alt
F.B.
F.B.
Hotel
F.B.
A59 ROAD
CANAL
CHURCH
Inn
STN
MAGHULL
To Liverpool
To Ormskirk

WALK No. 3

MAGHULL — SEFTON — LUNT — LITTLE CROSBY — CROSBY

DISTANCE:— 8 Miles **ALLOW:—** 5 Hours

START:— Maghull Railway Station **O.S. Ref:—** SD/383/015

This walk passes through several villages in the borough of Sefton.

From Maghull railway station, pass the Great Mogul Inn, and the shops, and then go forward to pass St. George's Church. Follow the main road left, and at the junction with Damfield Lane, cross the Leeds-Liverpool canal over the swing-bridge, and continue downhill to the crossroads.

Cross the road via the footbridge, and proceed along Hall Lane, to the half-timbered hotel, passing the playing field on your right.

At the junction, turn left, and using the right-hand pavement, take the first right turn into Ormonde Drive. Enter the path signposted "Netherton", and near the overhead cables, cross the footbridge.

Turn left and go up the steps. Enter the path ahead at the end of the fence, and take the path which leads slightly to the right, in the direction of Sefton church steeple.

On reaching a track, go left, and then downhill via a footbridge over the River Alt.

Go forward to pass the farm entrance, and enter Chapel Lane. Walk up the lane for about 200 yards, and then right, along a signposted track to a house.

At the house-front, go right for a few yards, and then turn left, to pass along the side fence of the house, along a fieldpath. Go forward along this path, to pass under the overhead electricity cables, crossing Netherton Brook via a footbridge.

On reaching a track, turn right, and follow the track, which meanders left and right, to the road at Sefton village (3a).

A left turn, and then the first right turn, takes you to Sefton Mill, the church, and the Punch Bowl Inn.

From the inn, proceed for about a mile along Lunt Road, in the direction of Ince Blundell, to the village of Lunt, keeping to the right-hand verge.

Continue along the road for a further half-mile, and on reaching a group of houses at a crossroads, turn left into Long Lane, in the direction of Thornton.

After about 300 yards, reach a long hedgerow leading off to the right, and enter here a signposted leafy path, from which you emerge at the wall of Ince Blundell Park.

Here, go left, and walk beside the wall along a lane to the main A565 road. At the road, cross carefully, go to the right, and after 100 yards, pass Sunnyfield Farm, and then turn left on to a track which runs along the edge of Moss Wood.

Follow this track to reach a gateway next to a house, at a road.

Go forward along the road, skirting the wall of Crosby Hall, to pass St. Mary's Church, Little Crosby, on your left.

At the crossroads in Little Crosby village (3b), go directly forward on to a sandy track, which takes you between the fields for a mile, to Hall Road East, and forward to our journey's end at Hall Road railway station in Crosby.

3a. SEFTON

The village of Sefton was mentioned in the Domesday Book. Before the Norman Conquest it was a Saxon settlement dating back to the 7th century. A church at Sefton, dedicated to St. Helen, was in existence before 1291. Before being transferred to the diocese of Liverpool in 1880, the parish was within the diocese of Lichfield, and then of Chester (1541). The church was rebuilt in 1552.

Sefton Hall, the seat of the Molyneux family, dating from the 14th century, stood opposite the south front of the church. Only a few of its stones now remain. In 1702 the Molyneux family moved to Croxteth Hall.

The church suffered slight internal damage caused by Cromwell's forces while they were billeted there.

Near the first cottage in the Thornton road, opposite and beyond the Punch Bowl Inn, is a spring of water known as St. Helen's Well. The Old Mill stands next to the churchyard wall.

3b. LITTLE CROSBY

The manor of Little Crosby was in the possession of the Molyneuxs from Norman times. In 1362 it passed by marriage to the Blundells. In the Civil War, William Blundell supported King Charles and raised an army containing some Crosby men. During the conflict he was imprisoned at Liverpool and his lands were confiscated. He repurchased them seven years later, and returned from exile in France on the same ship at Charles II, in whose reign William Blundell described Little Crosby as a small manor of about forty houses, and wrote that ". . . it had not a beggar, it had not an alehouse, it had not a Protestant in it".

The present church of St. Mary was built in 1847. In 1715 during the rebellion in support of the Stuart kings, a fruitless search of Crosby Hall was conducted while Nicholas Blundell hid in a secret passage.

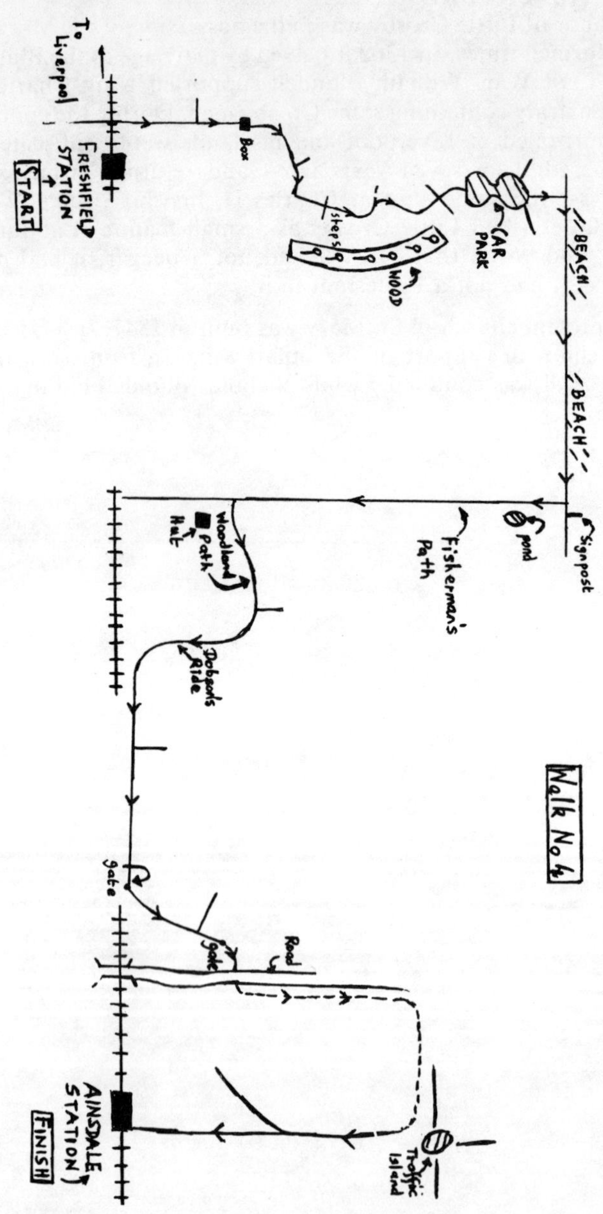

To Liverpool
FRESHFIELD STATION
START
Box
steps
WOOD
CAR PARK
BEACH
BEACH
Signpost
pond
Fisherman's Path
Woodland Path
Hut
Dobson's Ride
Walk No 4
gate
gate
Road
AINSDALE STATION
FINISH
Traffic Island

WALK No. 4

FRESHFIELD — FORMBY POINT — NATURE RESERVE — AINSDALE

DISTANCE:— 6 Miles **ALLOW:—** 4 Hours

START:— Freshfield Railway Station **O.S. Ref:—** SD/291/082

The Sefton Coast has one of the largest sand-dune systems in Britain. Part of this walk passes through the Ainsdale National Nature Reserve (4a).

From Freshfield station, set off on the signalbox side of the line, along tree-lined Victoria Road, in the direction of the beach.

After half a mile, pass Larkhill Lane and continue forward to enter the National Trust area of Formby Point. (Squirrels can occasionally be seen in their reserve in the woods to the left). Enter an avenue of pine trees ahead.

Take the first path on your right and enter "Cornerstone Walk". Keep to the main path. Turn right at the first path-junction, and using the white-topped posts as your guide, follow the path through the sandy woodland.

On reaching a crossroads of paths, go forward up the steps, following the whitened posts, along the edge of the tall pine-wood.

Continue to the end of the wood, and take to the stepped path over the dunes ahead, emerging at the car park.

Go forward and cross over the parking area to the boardwalk which is directly in front of you, and go forward along it, ignoring any paths to the left and right.

On reaching the beach, turn right, and walk along the sand at the shoreline in the direction of Southport, with the waters of Liverpool Bay at your left side.

Ignore any paths leading away from the beach, until, after about two miles, one reaches Fisherman's Path, clearly marked by a post and beacon.

Leave the beach by this path, and enter Ainsdale Nature Reserve (4a), over a boardwalk which passes to the right of a shallow pond.

Go forward to reach a path, and follow it through the duned woodland for about a mile.

Turn left to enter the signposted "Woodland Path", passing the ranger's hut.

Follow this path, skirting Formby Golf Course, to reach a T-junction. Here, do *not* turn left, but continue along the path signposted "Dobson's Ride".

This path eventually bears left, across a stretch of open ground, before reaching the railway lines.

Go along the path, with the woodland on your left side, for about a mile. Woodvale Airfield (4b) is in view to your right, beyond the railway.

Walk through two wide gateways and emerge at the coastal road.

Cross the road, and walk to the left, along the path by the fence, keeping the road to the left of you.

This path joins another one with white-topped posts. These are followed, until the sandy path over the dunes leads you through a small wood, to reach the road.

At the road, walk to the right, and follow the road, away from the beach, in the direction of Ainsdale village.

Continue past the Southport-Liverpool road junction, to arrive at Ainsdale railway station.

4a. AINSDALE NATIONAL NATURE RESERVE
The reserve is owned by the Nature Conservancy Council, and the land which it occupies was purchased in 1965. The main purpose of the reserve is nature conservation. Within the reserve there are six miles of public pathways, marked with white-topped posts.

The pine trees in the reserve were planted earlier in this century in order to shelter the farmland to the east, much of which lies below sea level at high tide.

Restoration of the dunes is being carried out, and is achieved by the building of brushwood fences to trap the wind-blown sand. Grasses are then planted in the dunes, which are thereby stabilised.

The dunes further north at Ainsdale, and at Birkdale, are managed in a similar way, as a local nature reserve.

4b. WOODVALE AIRFIELD

The airfield was a Royal Air Force base during the Second World War. At one period it housed two thousand personnel.

It is now used by a civilian aero club. R.A.F. cadets are trained there, and pilots of the Air Squadrons of the universities of Liverpool and Manchester.

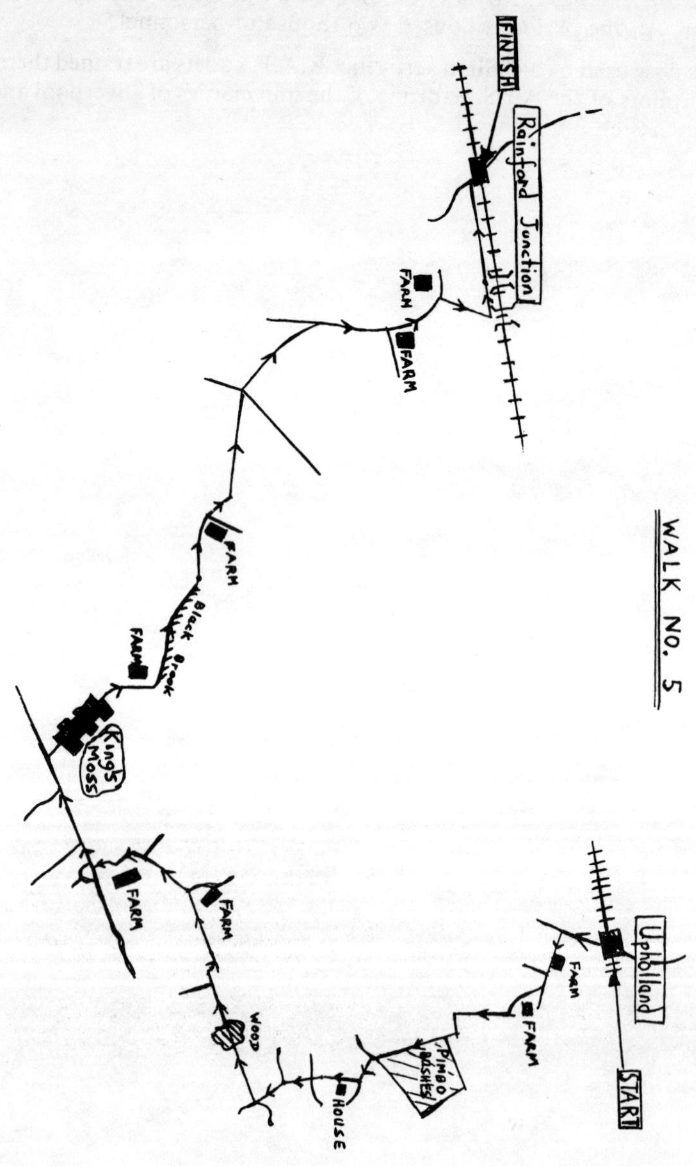
WALK NO. 5
START
Upholland
FARM
FARM
PIMBO BUSHES
HOUSE
WOOD
FARM
FARM
Kings Moss
FARM
Black Brook
FARM
FARM
FARM
Rainford Junction
FINISH

WALK No. 5

UPHOLLAND — PIMBO BUSHES — KING'S MOSS — RAINFORD

DISTANCE:— 7 Miles **ALLOW:—** 4 Hours

START:— Upholland Railway Station **O.S. Ref:—** SD/509/038

This walk crosses farmland on the edge of the old Orrell coalfield.

From Upholland station (5a), go downhill, along the main road via the left-hand pavement.

Ignore the first footpath sign on your left, and go forward, passing Pimbo Nurseries at your right side.

Fifty yards further on, turn left, on to a signposted lane leading to Higher Pimbo Farm.

Pass the first farm. Ignore the grassy lane on the left, and continue climbing up the lane to a junction. Here, take the right fork. The expanse of the Lancashire Plain then comes into view on your right.

Climb, with the trees on your left, and as you do so, excellent views across the plain can be seen.

Bear left, and near the gate ahead, enter the lane alongside it, and walk along the hedgerow, alongside Pimbo Bushes. The remains of old mine-workings are visible through a gap in the bushes. Walk along the track to pass a field on your left. Continue forward, and then turn left to go around the hedge ahead, into the next field.

Keep to the left hedge for about 30 yards and then turn right, walking over the large field in the direction of a house visible on the brow of the hill. The Wigan valley is in view on your left.

Bear left, to take the path going up alongside the house-fence.

Walk forward along the stony path, past the electricity pole. Descend a flight of steps and climb the flight opposite, and then cross a stile.

Climb to the crest of the hill, via a track to a gated stile. Cross the stile and immediately turn right, to walk down through a copse situated on old mine-workings. Descend along the right-hand hedge and cross a stile in the field-corner.

Continue down the right hedge of the next field to cross another stile, and then walk further down the hillside. Cross a stile, and then pass through a gateway on to a track.

Walk left along the track, and after about ¼ mile, reach a road junction. Here, take the right fork, away from the farm, to reach a road. Turn right, and continue along the road, walking downhill for ¾ mile to a T-junction. At the junction, turn right, and arrive at the village of King's Moss.

Bear right, along the road out to the far side of the village, to pass King's Moss Farm on your left. Just beyond this farm, turn left on to a signposted path, and then bear right to walk along the edge of Black Brook for ½ mile, finally keeping to the right-hand fence, and then alongside the ditch, to reach a lane by Moss House Farm.

Walk forward past the farm entrance, and follow the lane between the fields to a road at Reeds Brow. Turn left, past the entrance to the boarding kennels, and after about only 20 yards, turn right on to a grassy track.

The track takes you through the fields to Red House Farm, which is passed, the track then bearing left to a second farm called Maggots Nook. At the farm gates, turn right to reach a railway bridge.

At the bridge, take the footpath to the left. Walk down the steps and along the field-edge, with the railway line on your right side, to reach a second bridge. Continue in the same direction, alongside the railway fence for about half a mile, to emerge from the path at Rainford Junction station (5b).

5a. UPHOLLAND

The village is situated on the western edge of the Orrell coalfield. Over the years, more than a thousand shafts have been dug in order to reach the coal deposits around Wigan. The coalfield prospered after improvement work on the River Douglas was completed in 1742.

By making use of locks and artificial cuts, vessels were then able to export coal from Wigan and its surrounding pits, down the Douglas to the Ribble Estuary and Preston.

After the Leeds & Liverpool canal was linked to Wigan via the Douglas in 1779, the mining of coal proceeded on such a large scale that by the 1850's the Orrell Coalfield was to all intents and purposes exhausted.

Much of the coal had been used in Liverpool, which was growing rapidly at that time.

5b. RAINFORD
See Note 2a.

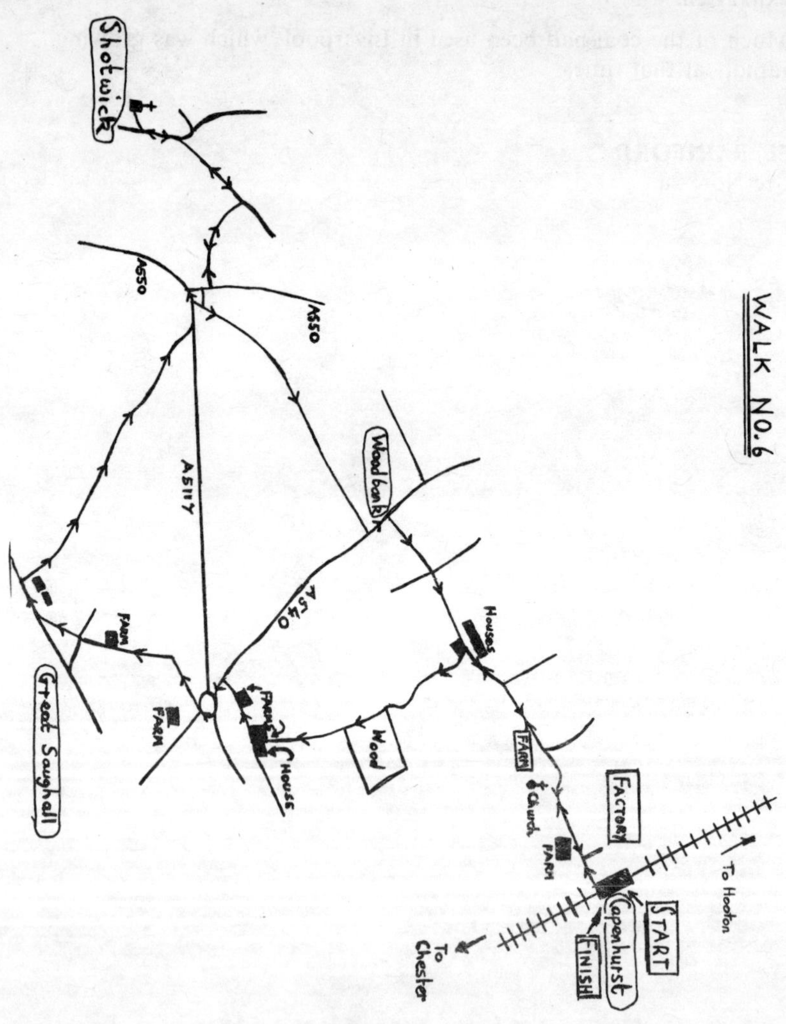
WALK NO.6
Shotwick
A550
A550
A5117
Woodbank
A540
Houses
Wood
FARM
FARMS
HOUSE
FARM
FARM
Great Saughall
Church
FARM
FARM
FACTORY
START
Capenhurst
FINISH
To Hooton
To Chester

WALK No. 6

CAPENHURST — GREAT SAUGHALL — SHOTWICK — WOODBANK — CAPENHURST

DISTANCE:— 9 Miles **ALLOW:—** 6½ Hours

START:— Capenhurst Railway Station **O.S. Ref:—** SJ/373/741

This walk passes through villages to the west of Chester.

From Capenhurst station, take the main road into the village, passing the British Nuclear Fuels factory on your right. The old buildings on your left are of Capenhurst Hall, which is now a farm. The parish church of Capenhurst and Ledsham is on your left.

Continue along the main road, passing the village green, and go forward into open country. Pass the buildings of Lower Brook Farm.

About 200 yards further on, look for a stile on the left, opposite a row of four small cottages. The stile is at the left side of the isolated Elm Cottage. This is the way to Great Saughall. Cross the footbridge and stile to enter the field.

Keep to the right-hand hedge, crossing any cattle-wire. Cross a series of fields via stiles. In the fourth field, still keep to the hedge and go over the stile. A large wooded area is to the left of you. Walk along the broad path at the right edge of the next long field, to the house visible ahead in the field corner. As you approach the house, look for Gibbet Windmill in the distance on the right.

Pass between the house and the buildings of Ashcroft Farm, along a leafy path to a road. Here, turn right, and pass the farm gate, continuing along the narrow road. Pass Rendova Farm to reach the main road.

At the road, turn left and walk along to the roundabout. Look ahead for a farm on the right with large red barns, situated on the far side of the roundabout. Carefully cross the two roads to reach this side. On the same roadside as the farm is a line of trees, just alongside the roundabout. Here, look for a green footpath signpost at a metal-railed fence.

Cross the stile and then the field, keeping to the left-hand hedge. Pass through the gateway, and then immediately turn left and walk along the left side of the next field. Cross the stile and continue in the same direction, going over the fields in the direction of the farm. The hills of North Wales can be seen to your right, across the River Dee.

At the side of the farm, cross the two stiles, and emerge at a lane. Walk left along the lane, past the houses to the small crossroads at Great Saughall.

Walk directly forward along Park Way, and at its end pass the police houses and walk ahead along a path which goes behind the churchyard wall. On reaching the school, walk left, to the main road.

At the road, turn right, pass the post-office, and walk downhill. After about 100 yards, look for a house called "Argoed". At the far side of this house is a signposted path. This is the path to Shotwick.

Climb the steps to the path and cross straight over the field to a wood. Cross the two stiles at the right side of the wide track, and walk ahead along the hedgerow. At the end of the field, turn left over a gated stile, and then immediately right, over a double stile with a connecting footbridge.

Go up the slope and across the next field, and then climb over the stile which is in front of you. Continue forward along the hedgerow. This fieldpath follows the direction of the River Dee, which is a couple of miles to your left, and good views of Clwyd can be seen along the way.

Walk over the undulating ground, crossing three stiles, and then a footbridge, in a hollow at the left corner of the next field.

Continue forward over the stile. (Do *not* turn left). Keep to the right-hand hedgerow alongside the ditch. Cross a further four stiles, pass over a wide track, and immediately turn right, and go over a double stile across the line of the hedge. Now walk to the left, keeping to the left-hand fence, towards the electricity pylon.

Cross a series of stiles, to reach the main A5117 road, alongside Bleak Farm. Carefully cross the road, and walk leftwards to the narrow minor road on your right, which is signposted "Woodbank". Pass across the entrance of this road, and then cross the A550 Birkenhead road, to enter a signposted footpath leading to Shotwick (6a).

Go diagonally to the right, over the field to a gate beyond the farm-paddock. The tower of Shotwick church nestles in the woodland to your left. Pass through the small metal gate, and then go immediately left through a larger gateway.

Walk down to the right, to the trees by Shotwick Brook, in the hollow, and pass through a small metal gate.

Cross the brook via the footbridge, and walk uphill, then over the next stile, to reach a lane. A left turn leads you to Shotwick village with its ancient church (6b).

Leave Shotwick by walking forward from the church gate and retracing your steps to the Woodbank road. Bear right and up the lane out of the village, and past the houses. Then cross the stile just past the derestriction signposts. Walk again over Shotwick Brook, and over the fields to the A550 road. Cross the road with care, and bear slightly to the right, to reach the opening of the narrow Woodbank Road.

A walk along this quiet road between the fields leads you out to the main A540 road at Woodbank.

Cross the road and walk to the left, past Delamere House, and some 30 yards along, turn right at a footpath signpost. Follow the path to reach a stile and a gateway. Cross the stile to a path which leads to Capenhurst.

Walk over the field and cross the double stile at the foot of the large tree. Continue along the left hedgerow to reach the Capenhurst road.

Bear right, along the main road, and then pass for a second time through Capenhurst village, and complete the walk at the railway station.

6a. SHOTWICK
See Note 1c.

6b. SHOTWICK CHURCH
See Note 1d.

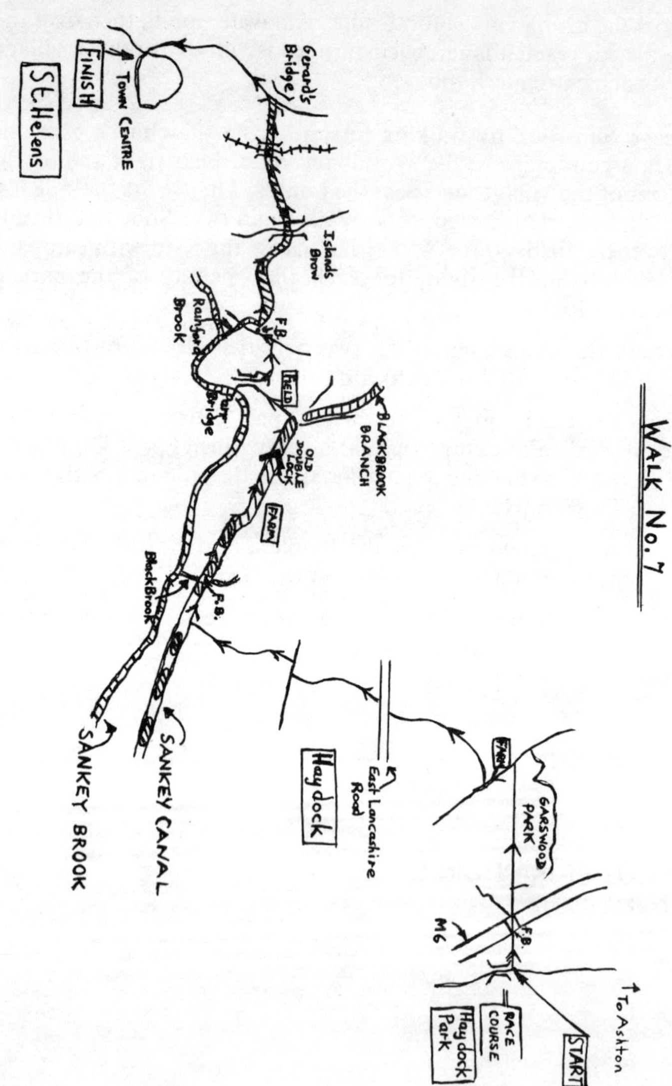
WALK No. 7
START
To Ashton
RACE COURSE
Haydock Park
F.B.
M6
GARSWOOD PARK
PARK
East Lancashire Road
Haydock
SANKEY CANAL
SANKEY BROOK
BlackBrook
F.B.
FARM
OLD DOUBLE LOCK
BLACKBROOK BRANCH
FIELD
Rainford Brook
F.B.
Islands Brow
Gerard's Bridge
TOWN CENTRE
FINISH
St. Helens

WALK No. 7

HAYDOCK PARK — GARSWOOD PARK — HAYDOCK — SANKEY CANAL — ST. HELENS

DISTANCE:— 7 Miles **ALLOW:—** 4½ Hours

START:— Haydock Park Racecourse **O.S. Ref:—** SJ/578/984

The walk follows waterways in the Upper Sankey Valley.

At the county boundary, enter a footpath situated 20 yards beyond the roadbridge opposite the entrance to Haydock Park racecourse.

Walk along with the wall at your right. After about 300 yards, bear slightly right and cross a footbridge over the M6 motorway. Go forward a few yards and turn right to follow the path at the right-hand edge of the field, alongside the boundary wall of Garswood Park.

A cottage comes into view ahead, with a banked reservoir to its left. At the end of the path, arrive at a road opposite Millfield Farm. Turn left along the road for about 100 yards, to reach a T-junction. Cross the road and enter Haydock Lane.

After the road swings to the left, go down the hill, with open farmland to your right and St. Helens lying below. Pass an industrial estate and reach the East Lancashire Road.

Carefully cross the dual-carriageway and walk down the second part of Haydock Lane. Pass the landscaped mine-workings, with Clipsley Brook flowing along at your right.

As the lane widens, it winds to and fro, to reach Clipsley Lane. At the T-junction, cross over and walk to the right for about 50 yards, and then turn left into Cooper Lane.

Walk downhill past the houses. At the entrance to Station Road, go forward into a lane. At the first gateway on the left, Newton-le-Willows can be seen in the wooded area across the fields.

Go forward down the path, which runs between a hedgerow and an embankment, into the Sankey Valley.

On reaching a crosspath, turn right, and follow the path alongside the Sankey Canal (7a). Beyond the canal the Sankey Brook flows below an embankment. Walking along the wide path, one passes several watered sections of the canal.

Cross the footbridge at the site of Engine Lock. Follow the path between the line of the canal and the Sankey Brook, to reach a weir. Black Brook crosses the canal and flows into Sankey Brook.

At the end of the next watered section of the canal, bear slightly right to reach a wide towing-path. Callen's Farm stands on the right, beyond the canal. Walk forward for about 100 yards to reach a cascade. This is the site of the Old Double Lock.

Go ahead to reach a field, where the Blackbrook branch of the canal winds away northwards to your right.

Turn left, and walk away from the canal, along the extreme left boundary fence of the field. The path swings gradually to the right, along the side of Sankey Brook, to reach a road at Parr Bridge.

To rejoin the main line of the canal, cross the road and turn right. Walk along to reach Blackbrook Road at a T-junction. Turn left past the public house, and after 100 yards cross the road to a footbridge over a weir.

At this point the canal used to join Rainford Brook, which now flows over the weir. Cross the footbridge and follow the path along the left side of the canal below a landscaped area of grass. The path widens to reach the road at Islands Brow.

Cross the road and enter the wide path which runs along the right-hand edge of the canal. Pass along a deep cutting and then under a railway bridge to arrive at a road at Gerard's Bridge.

Turn left and walk along College Street to complete the walk at St. Helens town centre.

7a. THE SANKEY CANAL
See Note 9a.

WALK No. 8

A59
Canal
Hall
B5246
Ruffor
START
To Burscough
ditch
Farm
MILL
FARM
Tarlscough
Wildfowl
Reserve
Martin
Mere
Building
Works
Railway
Burscough
Canal
FINISH
Bridge
32

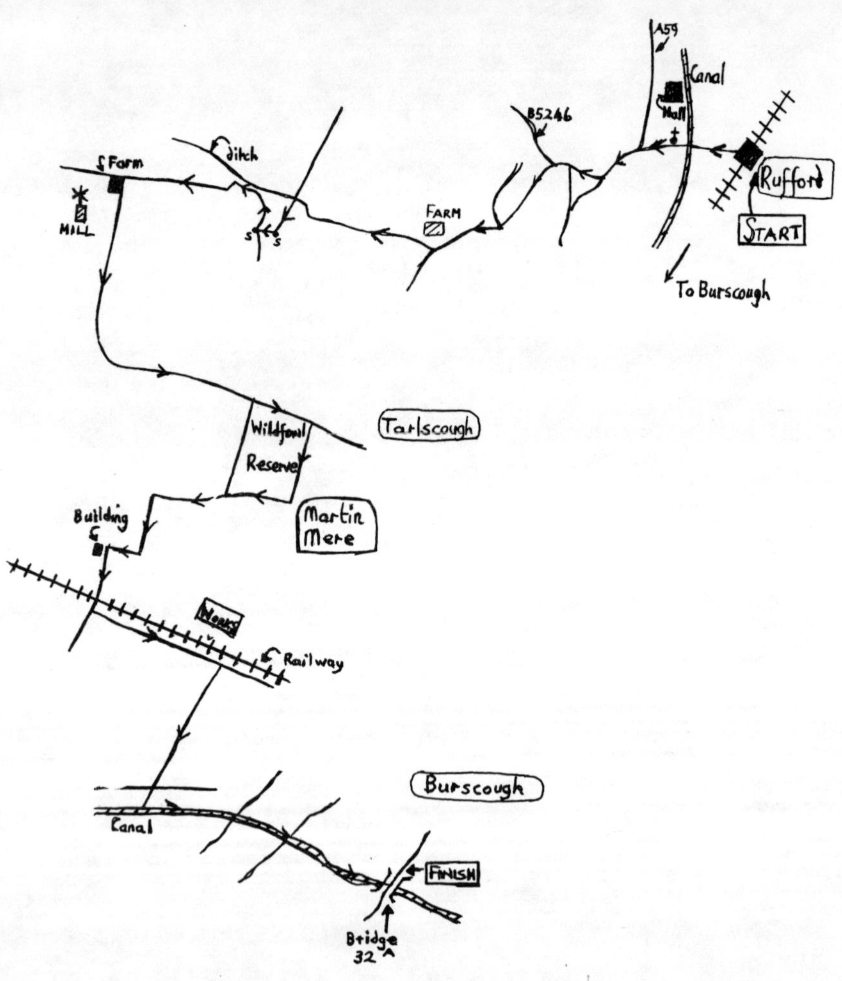

WALK No. 8

RUFFORD — TARLSCOUGH MOSS — MARTIN MERE — LEEDS & LIVERPOOL CANAL — BURSCOUGH

DISTANCE:— $8\frac{1}{2}$ Miles **ALLOW:—** 6 Hours

START:— Rufford Railway Station **O.S. Ref:—** SD/467/157

The first section of this walk is across the rich agricultural land to the west of the River Douglas. The final part takes you along the towing-path of the Leeds & Liverpool Canal.

From Rufford railway station (8a), begin by walking in the direction of the church. Cross the Rufford branch of the Leeds & Liverpool canal (8b) via the narrow humped bridge.

After passing Rufford parish church (8c), continue along the main road, to reach the A59 Liverpool-Preston road. Turn and walk to the left along the line of the old road, which is now a lay-by.

After about 100 yards, cross the road, and enter the B5246 Holmeswood road, which is signposted "Southport".

Walk past the village school, which was built in 1824, and then turn left into Brick Kiln Lane. A few minutes of walking brings you towards open country.

Pass across the entrance to Brick Kiln Farm, and walk along the road, with the line of trees to your left.

The road swings to the right, past Sunnyfields Cottage, and when you reach this point, go left along Tootle Lane, to walk across the flat open country of Tarlscough Moss. The last isolated set of buildings which you pass are of Tootle House Farm. The expanse of Mere Sands Wood lies to the right.

At the road-junction by the farm, bear right, along Mere Lane. As you approach Helm House Farm, the tower of an old windmill comes into view ahead of you in the distance. As you proceed across the level country, the village of Holmeswood lies a couple of miles over to your right. Looking back, the hills of the Parbold and Wigan areas can be seen to the east.

On reaching a line of trees, where the road swings to the right, turn left in front of the hedgerow, and walk along it.

Cross the footbridge, turn right, and walk some 50 yards, towards a second footbridge, carefully avoiding the drainage ditch to your right.

Cross over the second footbridge (do *not* turn left), and walk forward along the bank of the ditch. After 20 yards or so, turn left, and then right, to avoid any flooded land, and then go forward to the gap in the hedge and cross a wide signposted bridge. Walk along the left-hand boundary of the next field, over the peaty ground, towards the road at the right side of the windmill and the farm buildings.

On emerging at the road, turn left, and pass Windmill Farm, keeping to the right-hand verge. You are now walking in the direction of Martin Mere, and of the adjoining hamlet of Tarlscough.

After half a mile, the road swings leftwards and continues alongside Martin Mere Wildfowl Reserve (8d). A large expanse of lawn, and several picnic areas are available in front of the main entrance to the reserve.

From the front entrance, turn right, along the road in the direction of Burscough. After passing about 100 yards of the hedgerow, turn right, down a track which runs alongside the boundary fence of the reserve.

Keep alongside the fence, and then turn right, and walk along the rear fence of the enclosed area, using a wide grassy track.

At the end of the tree-lined fence, go directly forward to cross two bridges, and then continue ahead along the track, on to open ground.

After about 200 yards, enter a track on the left, and walk along the left fence of the field to a stile.

Cross the stile and go forward from it, to reach the end of the field. Turn right, and walk for about 100 yards, towards the right-hand edge of the old building, with the ditch to the left of you.

Turn left at the building, pass in front of it, and walk along a track to the railway level crossing.

Having crossed the railway, turn sharp left, and walk alongside the railway fence via an old track, in the direction of New Lane station.

After about half a mile, one reaches a line of trees, visible across the railway, beyond which there is a sewage farm. Just past the farm boundary, a broad track leads to the right.

Follow this track. Several large farm buildings are visible ahead on the skyline. The track reaches a tarmac road.

Here, go forward to reach the Leeds & Liverpool Canal. Do not cross the canal swing-bridge, but instead, turn left and walk along the towing-path.

A couple of miles of easy walking completes the walk at the stone roadbridge, numbered 32A, at Burscough (8e).

8a. RUFFORD

The Rufford branch of the Leeds & Liverpool canal runs from a point east of Burscough to the River Ribble — a distance of 7¼ miles.

A few minutes walk from the village, stands Rufford Old Hall, built around 1490. It was donated to the National Trust by the Hesketh family in 1936. The building was added to in 1662, and in 1821. The Hall is open to the public. A village museum is housed in rooms of the 1821 wing. A building known as Rufford New Hall stands in parkland, and is now separated from the Old Hall by the main A59 road. It was built in 1760, enlarged in 1798, and is now used as a hospital.

8b. THE LEEDS & LIVERPOOL CANAL

The canal runs from the Aire and Calder Navigation at Leeds to the River Mersey via Stanley Dock, a distances of 127¼ miles. A branch runs from the main line canal for three miles to Rufford, and then into the tideway of the River Douglas at Tarleton, a further 4¼ miles away. The 28-mile section of the canal from Liverpool to Parbold was completed in 1774. The line was extended to Wigan by 1779, and the Rufford branch was finished in 1781.

The final section of the canal was finished in 1816, some 46 years after parliament had authorised its construction.

8c. RUFFORD PARISH CHURCH

The church was built in 1869 on the site of an older chapel built in 1736, which became the parish church when Rufford was separated from the parish of Croston in 1793. On a wall inside the church there is a memorial to Sir William Hesketh, bearing a verse composed by the English poet William Cowper, who was related by marriage to the Hesketh family.

8d. MARTIN MERE

The Martin Mere Wildfowl Reserve was established in 1975 by the Wildfowl Trust. Before the land was drained, Martin Mere was the name given to a large lake which stretched from Rufford, westwards as far as Crossens near Southport. It was the biggest lake in Lancashire. Until 1700, the Mere drained into the River Douglas at Rufford. In the winter months at that time, the Douglas flowed into the Mere and thereby increased its area. Work to drain the lake into the Ribble estuary at Crossens began in 1692. In 1853, a steam-pump was introduced, with the result that the land was flooded only in the winter months.

In periods of exceptionally heavy rainfall, flooding can still occur, but a new pumping-station, opened at Crossens in 1961, has now made flooding less likely.

Before draining, Martin Mere was an abundant source of fish for the locality, and part of the fishing rights were held by nearby Burscough Priory.

The rich agricultural land in the locality was formed by the build-up of peat on the bed of the lake over a long period of time.

8e. BURSCOUGH

In Burscough, a priory used to stand about halfway between Burscough Junction and Ormskirk stations, on the east side of the railway, near Abbey Farm. It was founded around 1190 by the Augustinian order of monks. Following the dissolution of the monasteries in 1536 it fell into decay, and at the present time, various pieces of masonry lie on the spot where it once stood.

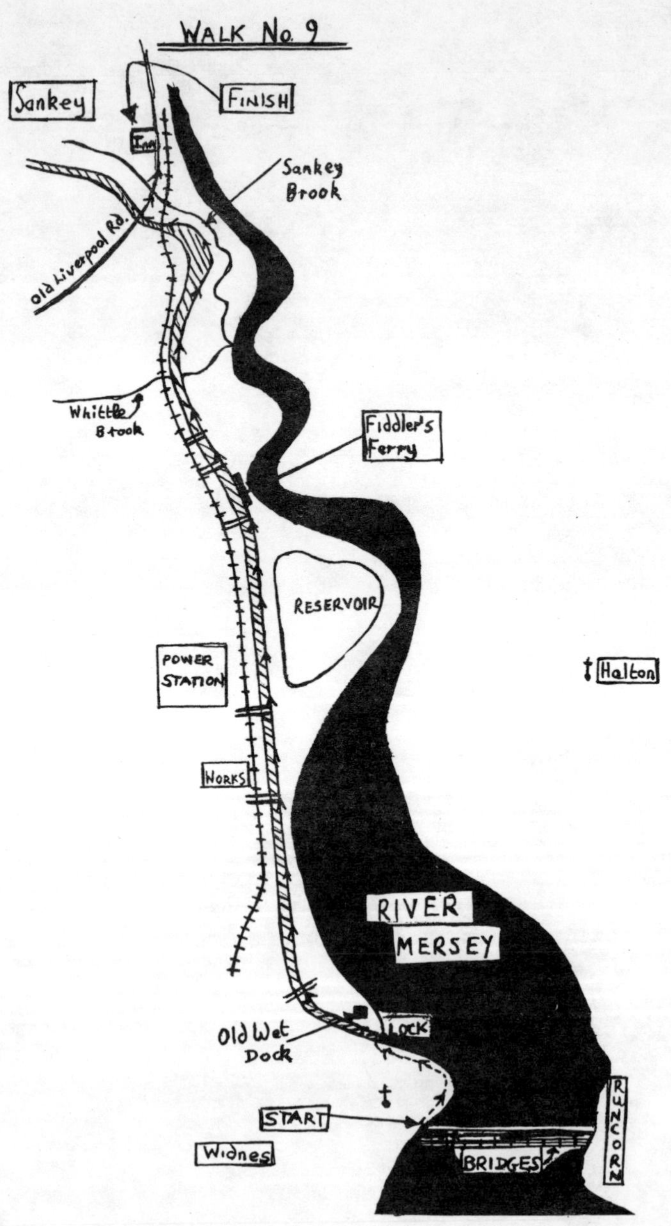
WALK No. 9
Sankey
FINISH
Inn
Sankey Brook
Old Liverpool Rd.
Whittle Brook
Fiddler's Ferry
RESERVOIR
POWER STATION
Halton
WORKS
RIVER MERSEY
LOCK
Old Wet Dock
START
Widnes
BRIDGES
RUNCORN

WALK No. 9

WIDNES — FIDDLER'S FERRY — SANKEY BRIDGES

DISTANCE:— 6 Miles **ALLOW:—** 4 Hours

START:— Widnes (West Bank) **O.S. Ref:—** SJ/511/837

This walk follows the towing-path of the Sankey Canal. It also passes along the shore of the upper reaches of the Mersey estuary.

Begin the walk at West Bank in Widnes, at the end of Victoria Promenade, close to the two bridges.

The oldest part of Runcorn lies directly across the Mersey from this point.

Walk to the left along the promenade, and at its end, turn left to pass through the public gardens into St. Mary's Road. Turn right, and walk past the church. At the end of the road, enter a pathway which leads you leftwards, to a grassy area of parkland known as Spike Island.

Ahead is the end of the Sankey Canal (9a). A large lock connects it to the river. Cross over the canal via a footbridge alongside the lock.

Enter a path situated some yards from the canal-edge, and arrive at the Old West Dock (9b), which has a slipway connecting it to the river.

Walk along the pathway leading away from the river and parallel to the canal. On reaching the small wooden footbridge, continue forward along the towing-path, on the right-hand edge of the canal. The path leads you forward between the canal and the Mersey shore, towards Fiddler's Ferry.

On this part of the walk the contrast between the industrial and rural landscapes is sharp. On your left is a chemical works, and the cooling-towers of the power station lie ahead in the distance. Across the Mersey on the Cheshire side, the spire of Halton church is visible on the summit of a steep hill.

Pass a footbridge and a signal box to continue forward. Here the river widens, and the shoreline begins to curve away to the right. Across and beyond the river lies the Manchester Ship Canal. Vessels can often be seen making their way towards Weston Point Dock and Ellesmere Port, further downstream.

After a half-mile or so, one passes Fiddler's Ferry power station. A large reservoir protected by floodbanks lies to the right.

Near the power station the canal narrows, and after about 200 yards returns to its original width. In the distance, the spire of the church at Sankey Bridges comes into view as one approaches Fiddler's Ferry.

Just before reaching the modern factory, an isolated cottage can be seen on the shore. The ferry-boats have long ago ceased to ply to and fro from this point, but many craft still use it as an anchorage, and are able to pass between the river and the canal via a lock and a slipway. Just beyond the boatyard, the Ferry Tavern faces the river along a lane to the right.

Go forward to resume the walk to Sankey. A modern housing development at Penketh is passed, and the towing-path crosses Whittle Brook via a footbridge.

About ¾ mile further, one passes a footbridge, to reach a point where the canal swings sharply leftwards.

Cross the Sankey Brook, and then walk carefully over the railway track via a level crossing. After about 100 yards one reaches Sankey Bridges at Old Liverpool Road.

Just across the road is a large recreation and picnic area set in extensive parkland on both sides of the canal.

A bus can be boarded for Widnes or Liverpool at the Sloop Inn, which is on Old Liverpool Road, about fifty yards on the Warrington side of the Canal.

9a. THE SANKEY CANAL

The canal was the first artificially constructed British waterway to be independent of tidal waters. It was opened three years before the Duke of Bridgewater's canal, and is also known as the St. Helens Canal.

The first section, from a point on Sankey Brook, below Sankey Bridges, to Parr near St. Helens, was opened in 1757. The original purpose of the canal was the carriage of coal to the Mersey from collieries in the Parr district.

In 1762 it was extended to Fiddler's Ferry, at which point vessels could pass into the Mersey via a lock. The canal was extended to Widnes in 1833.

As well as improving the export of coal, the Sankey Canal helped to open up the St. Helens district as a centre for the manufacture of glass and chemicals.

In 1931, a portion below St. Helens was closed, and its whole length was completely disused by 1959.

9b. THE OLD WET DOCK

The final extension of the canal from Fiddler's Ferry to Widnes was begun in 1830. After its completion, vessels were able to pass between the canal and the Mersey via a lock at West Bank which operated from 1833. The sides of the canal were strengthened and paved, to form moorings. The site was linked to a railway running from St. Helens.

A more modern dock on West Bank was opened in 1862, but this has long ago been filled in. It was connected by a private railway to a line running through Widnes from Warrington to Garston.

In 1847 John Hutchinson established his factory for the manufacture of soda on a site between the canal and the river. He can be regarded as the founder of the Widnes chemical industry.

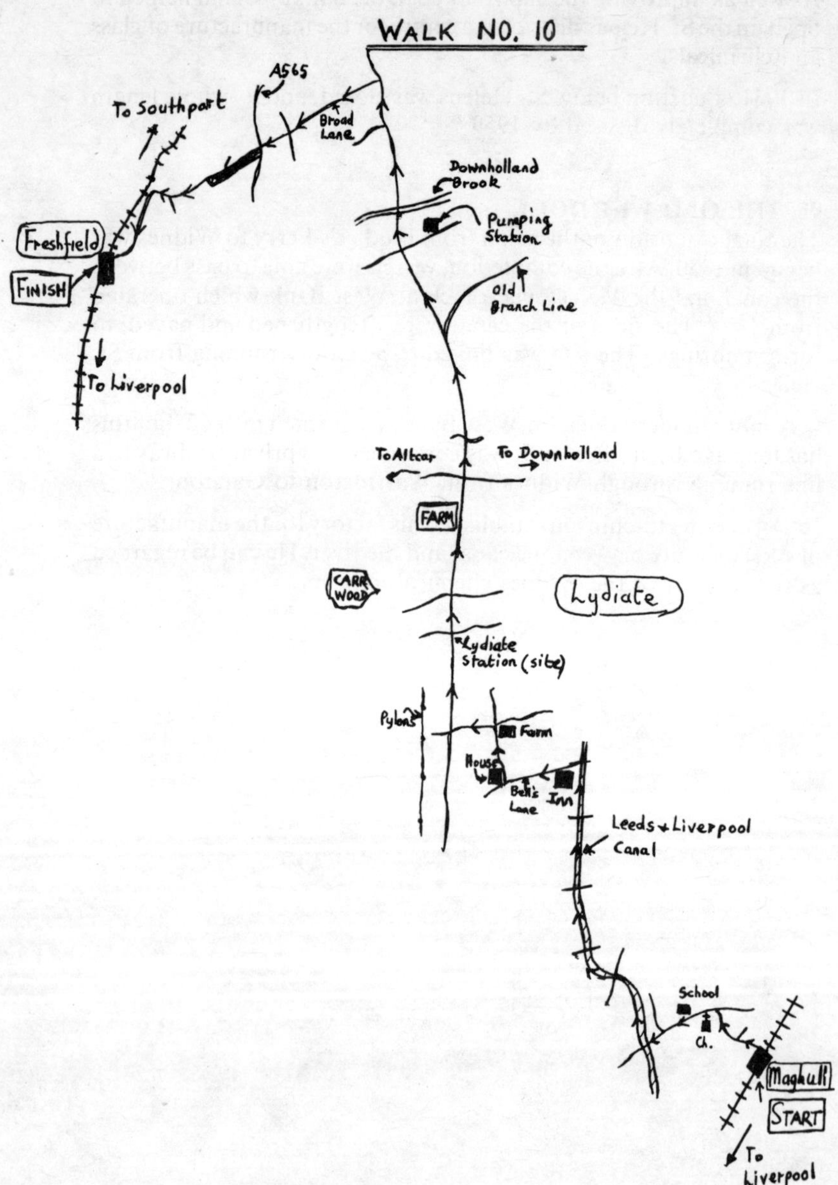
WALK NO. 10
A565
To Southport
Broad Lane
Downholland Brook
Pumping Station
Freshfield
FINISH
Old Branch Line
To Liverpool
To Altcar
To Downholland
FARM
CARR WOOD
Lydiate
Lydiate Station (site)
Pylons
Farm
House
Bell's Lane
Inn
Leeds + Liverpool Canal
School
Ch.
Maghull
START
To Liverpool

WALK No. 10

MAGHULL — LEEDS & LIVERPOOL CANAL — ALTCAR — DOWNHOLLAND MOSS — FRESHFIELD

DISTANCE:— 10 Miles **ALLOW:—** 6½ Hours

START:— Maghull Railway Station **O.S. Ref:—** SD/383/015

A large part of this walk passes through isolated country, along the course of a dismantled railway line (10a), and also along the towing-path of the Leeds & Liverpool canal (10b).

Starting from the railway station at Maghull, turn right, and walk past the Great Mogul Inn, and continue ahead, to pass St. George's Church on the left. At the road-junction, turn left, to pass a school, and, where the road swings to the right, go directly forward to cross the Leeds & Liverpool canal via a swing-bridge.

Turn right, on to the towing-path, and continue your journey out of Maghull in the direction of Lydiate, passing a sports field on your left.

As one walks along the path, open country comes into view. On reaching the swing-bridge alongside the Running Horses Inn, leave the towing-path by turning left, to walk down Bell's Lane.

The spire of Sefton church is visible in the distance on your left. After about ¼ mile, the road swings right, into Altcar Lane, and one reaches a cottage displaying a mason's inscription dated 1596.

When you reach a T-junction opposite a farm, turn left, and walk down an old lane to a crosspath. Here, turn right, and walk along the footpath, where a railway track used to run. A line of electricity pylons follows the direction of the path, running parallel to it, some distance away to the left.

Just beyond the next crosspath is the site of Lydiate station. The woodlands at the left-hand horizon are on estates at Ince Blundell and at Little Crosby. Closer to you on the left is Carr Wood, and the area of land around it is known locally as Altcar Meadows (10c).

After passing alongside the boundary fence of a modern sewage farm, walk under a bridge, which carries the road from Altcar to Downholland.

Pass under the second bridge of three arches. The right-hand arch spans a wide drainage ditch. This ditch is known as the Cheshire Lines Brook, and water is pumped along it, and out into the River Alt, via a network of interconnected channels.

About a mile further along the path, one arrives at a large patch of open ground, from which the path of an old branch-line runs off to the right.

Here, continue in your original direction, forward along the track, crossing the area of Downholland Moss.

About ¼ mile further on, pass a metal bridge, which carries two large water pipes, and after a similar distance, walk through a gateway and then under a roadbridge. The track then widens into a road, which leads you forward to cross a bridge over Downholland Brook. Traces of the old rail track can be seen on the right-hand portion of the bridge.

Go along the cindered track, to reach a T-junction. Continue forward through a gateway, to cross the length of field ahead of you, alongside the left-hand boundary fence. At the end of the field, turn left, into Broad Lane. Walk along this lane in the direction of Freshfield, on the final stage of the walk.

As the Mersey coast is approached, the earth becomes more sandy. Walk along the lane, between the fields, to reach a narrow road.

Cross over and walk along a short stretch of tarmac to reach the main A565 road. Carefully cross the road, and enter a path at the right of the houses.

This narrow path leads you past a riding-school, to emerge at Kenton Close.

Here, turn right, and then sharply to the left, into Brewery Lane. A little further on, the lane widens to form a road.

Go forward, ignoring a signposted footpath on your left. Where the road swings leftwards, enter a footpath signposted "Montagu Road".

The woodland of the Ainsdale Nature Reserve is visible on the right. At the fence-corner, ignore the path to the left. Instead, go slightly to the right, and then immediately left, towards the railway line, over part of Freshfield Heath.

At the railway, turn left, into Montagu Road. By walking past Fisherman's Close, and then along a short stretch of bridlepath, one soon arrives at Freshfield railway station.

10a. THE CHESHIRE LINES RAILWAY

The walk from Maghull is along the line of the Aintree to Southport (Lord Street) railway. It was opened to traffic in 1884 by the Cheshire Lines and Southport Extension Railway Company. It was a double line track. After 1889 it was operated by the Cheshire Lines Committee.

A branch line from Altcar & Hillhouse Junction connected with Preston via Southport Central. The stations between Aintree and Lord St. were Sefton & Maghull, Lydiate, Altcar & Hillhouse, Mossbridge, Woodvale, Ainsdale Beach, and Birkdale Palace.

Altcar & Hillhouse station was opened in 1887, and the service between there and Southport Central was known locally as the "Altcar Bob".

It continued to be run by the Cheshire Lines Committee until the nationalisation of the railways in 1948. The line was closed in 1952 and the track removed.

10b. THE LEEDS AND LIVERPOOL CANAL

See Note 8b.

10c. ALTCAR

Altcar is the traditional venue of the Waterloo Cup, which is awarded annually to the owner of the champion greyhound at a hare-coursing meeting. The cup was first awarded in 1836, and the meeting takes place each February on various courses in and around Altcar.

PUBLIC TRANSPORT INFORMATION

AINSDALE
Merseyrail Northern Line
(Liverpool Cen. — Southport)

AUGHTON (TOWN GREEN)
Merseyrail Northern Line
(Liverpool Cen. — Ormskirk)

BURSCOUGH
(1) Merseyrail Northern Line
(Liverpool Cen. — Ormskirk)
(2) British Rail
(Ormskirk — Preston)

CAPENHURST
(1) Merseyrail Wirral Line
(Liverpool Cen. — Hooton)
(2) British Rail
(Hooton — Chester)

CROSBY (HALL ROAD)
Merseyrail Northern Line
(Liverpool Cen. — Southport)

FRESHFIELD
Merseyrail Northern Line
(Liverpool Cen. — Southport)

HAYDOCK PARK
Manchester Transport Bus 320
(Liverpool — Wigan)

HOOTON
Merseyrail from Liverpool Central

MAGHULL
Merseyrail Northern Line
(Liverpool Cen. — Ormskirk)

RAINFORD
(1) Merseyrail Northern Line
(Liverpool Cen. — Kirkby)
(2) British Rail
(Kirkby — Wigan Wallgate)

RUFFORD
(1) Merseyrail Northern Line
(Liverpool Cen. — Ormskirk)
(2) British Rail
(Ormskirk — Preston)

SANKEY BRIDGES
Crosville Bus H5
(Warrington — Liverpool)

ST. HELENS
Merseyrail City Line
(Liverpool Lime St. — Wigan)

or

Merseybus 10/10A
(Liverpool — St. Helens)

or

Manchester Transport Bus 320
(Liverpool — Wigan)

UPHOLLAND
(1) Merseyrail Northern Line
(Liverpool Cen. — Kirkby)
(2) British Rail
(Kirkby — Wigan Wallgate)

WIDNES (WEST BANK)
Crosville Town Lynx Bus X5
(Liverpool — Runcorn)

OTHER TITLES FROM

Countyvise

Local History
Birkenhead Priory £1.80
The Spire is Rising £1.95
The Search for Old Wirral £9.95
Birkenhead Park £1.40
A Guide to Merseyside's Industrial Past £1.95
Neston and Parkgate £2.00
Scotland Road £5.95
Helen Forrester Walk £1.00
Women at War £2.95
Merseyside Moggies £1.00
Dream Palaces £7.50
The Liverpool Competition (Local Cricket) £2.95

Local Shipping Titles
Sail on the Mersey £1.95
The Mersey at Work — Ferries £1.40
Ghost Ships on the Mersey £1.40
The Liners of Liverpool - *Part I* £2.95
The Liners of Liverpool - *Part II* £2.95

Local Railway Titles
Seventeen Stations to Dingle £2.95
The Line Beneath the Liners £2.95
Steel Wheels to Deeside £2.95
Seaport to Seaside £4.25
Northern Rail Heritage £1.95
A Portrait of Wirral's Railways £3.95

History with Humour
The One-Eyed City £2.95
Hard Knocks £3.95
The Binmen are coming £3.50

Other Titles
Speak through the Earthquake, Wind & Fire £3.95
It's Me, O Lord £0.40
Companion to the Fylde £1.75
Bird Watching in Cheshire £3.95